EGYPTIAN HISTORY

Understanding ancient Egypt

By: **Harold J. Ruiz**

Table of contents

……..Egyptian beliefs.

……..Egyptian gods.

……..Egyptian Architecture.

……..Egyptian art.

Chapter 1

Egyptian beliefs

The polytheistic ancient Egyptians held that forces in the natural, supernatural, and human worlds were governed by gods and goddesses. The abstract idea of maat, which was symbolized by the goddess Maat and is frequently translated as "truth," "justice," and "cosmic order," served as the fundamental ruling force in traditional Egyptian thought. The living were required to constantly worship and offer sacrifices to the gods in order to appease the gods and spirits of the afterlife, or maat.

The ancient Egyptians thought that a person's spirit was immortal provided they were properly prepared for the afterlife. The soul, often referred to as ka, follows a person throughout their entire existence before departing from the body after death to enter the afterlife. Without a body, an individual's ka would not be possible. The purpose of elaborate funeral ceremonies and rituals, including as tomb construction, mummification, and funerary rites, was to prepare the body and the spirit for the hereafter.

A mother, a father, and a kid made up many of the gods and goddesses that made up the Egyptian pantheon, which was made up of them. Each deity or goddess had a connection to one or more locations where large temples had been erected to hold their statues. Egypt's gods and goddesses had a wide variety of appearances. In Egyptian art, many were shown with both human and animal features. Horus, the deity of the sky, battle, and protection, frequently assumes a human body with a falcon's head. Others were presented as supernatural people. Osiris, for instance, was pictured as a man with a face that was either black (referential to the rich Nile soil) or green (referential to the afterlife's judges of the dead) (representing new life). Numerous Egyptian deities were also linked to traits or tools that they used to carry out their divine functions. For instance, the goddess of magic and maternity Isis was frequently depicted clutching an ankh or a lotus.

The pharaoh, who was regarded as semi-divine and was credited with mediating between people and the gods, held the greatest position in Egyptian society.

Egyptian civilization during that time period was deeply ingrained with religious ideas and customs (from c. 3000 BCE). Although there are undoubtedly many remnants of prehistory, they may not be very significant for understanding subsequent periods because the changes that brought about the establishment of the Egyptian state gave religion a new setting.

It is not useful to see religion as a single thing that cohered as a system because religious occurrences were so prevalent. However, it is important to consider religion in light of possibly nonreligious human behaviors and principles. The emphasis and practices of Egyptian religion changed significantly throughout the course of its more than 3,000-year history, yet the religion's personality and aesthetic were consistently consistent throughout.

It is incorrect to characterize religion as being limited to the worship of deities and human piety. Contact with the dead, rituals like oracles and divination, and magic, which largely relied on divine tools and associations, all fell under the category of religious behavior.

King and the gods were the two main focuses of public religion. Both rank among the most defining characteristics of Egyptian culture. The monarch enjoyed a special position between humans and the gods, participated in their realm, and built impressive monuments to honor him in the afterlife for religious reasons. Egyptian deities are well known for their vast range of appearances, which includes human and animal hybrid forms. The sun god, who went by many names and personas and was connected to a wide variety of supernatural creatures in a solar cycle based on the alternation of night and day, and Osiris, the god of the dead and lord of the underworld, were the most significant deities. During the first millennium BCE, when solar worship was comparatively on the decrease, Osiris and Isis rose to prominence in a variety of circumstances.

The gods and the current world—whose center, of course, was Egypt—were included in the Egyptian conception of the universe, which was also surrounded by the chaotic world from which order had emerged and would eventually return. It was necessary to prevent chaos. As the principal figure in human civilization, the king had the responsibility of upholding the goodness of the gods in preserving order against chaos. This ultimately pessimistic understanding of the universe was primarily connected to the solar cycle and the sun god. It gave the king and aristocracy a strong sense of justification for maintaining order.

Despite this pessimism, the official depiction of the universe on the monuments was optimistic and positive, representing the king and the gods in unbroken reciprocity. The flimsy order was reinforced by this implicit contrast. The constrained nature of the monuments was essential to a decorum system that established what could be seen, how it might be shown, and in what setting. The upholding of decorum and order strengthened one another.

Chapter 2

Egyptian gods

Ancient Egyptians' daily life were deeply influenced by the gods and goddesses. Therefore, it is hardly unexpected that the Egyptian pantheon contained more than 2,000 gods. Isis, Osiris, Horus, Amun, Ra, Hathor, Bastet, Thoth, Anubis, and Ptah are some of these gods' well-known names; many others are less well-known.

While other gods were connected to a particular region or, in certain circumstances, a ritual or position, the more well-known ones became state deities. For instance, Seshat was the goddess of written words and precise measurements who was overshadowed by Thoth, the more well-known god of writing and patron of scribes. The goddess Qebhet was a little-known deity who provided cool water to the souls of the deceased as they awaited judgment in the afterlife.

Understanding these gods and their crucial role in every person's immortal journey led to the development of ancient Egyptian culture.

The gods developed into a highly anthropomorphic and magical belief system from an animistic one. In addition to being the god of magic and healing, Heka was also the primal power that enabled creation and supported both human and divine life. Heka existed before all other gods.

Ma'at, which stands for harmony and balance and is symbolized by the goddess of the same name and her white ostrich feather, was the cornerstone of Egyptian culture. Heka strengthened Ma'at, just as he did all the other gods. Heka was a manifestation of heka (magic), which is best understood as natural rules that, to us now, would be regarded as supernatural but, to the Egyptians, were merely the way that the world and the cosmos worked. All beneficial things were given to humanity by the gods, but heka made it possible for them to use them.

All of these gods had names, distinct personalities and traits, wore various dress types, revered various objects, ruled over distinct spheres of influence, and responded to events in a highly unique manner. Each deity had a specialty, but they were frequently connected to several aspects of human life.

For instance, Hathor was a goddess of music, dance, and inebriation who was also regarded as an old Mother Goddess. She was also connected to the Milky Way, which was thought to be a divine mirror of the Nile River, and was a destroyer in her former life as Sekhmet. Originally a goddess of war, Neith evolved into the ideal Mother Goddess, a loving figure who the gods would consult in order to resolve their conflicts. Many deities, including Set and Serket, changed over time to assume new functions and obligations.

The main gods and what they stood
for are listed below.

An early moon god called A'ah later
became Iah (also known as Yah) and
then Khonsu.

Aken was in charge of the vessel that
transported dead people from Lily
Lake to the Field of Reeds in the
afterlife. He slept until Hraf-Hef, the
grumpy Divine Ferryman, needed him.
Only the Book of the Dead contains a
mention of his name.

The eastern and western horizons of
the afterlife are protected by Aker, the
deified horizon. At dawn and sunset,
he guarded Ra's sun barge as it
entered and exited the underworld.

Am-Heh was a demonic being who resided in a lake of fire and was known as the "devourer of millions" and the "eating of eternity."

Amenet (Amentet) was a goddess who provided food and drink to the deceased as they entered the afterlife. Amenet, also referred to as "She of the West," was the Divine Ferryman's spouse. She made her home in a tree close to the underworld's entrances. Hathor and Horus's child.

Ammit (Ammut) is a goddess known as the "Devourer of Souls" who had the head, torso, and hindquarters of a crocodile, leopard, and hippo. She ate the hearts of those souls who Osiris had not been able to justify as she sat beneath the scales of justice in the Hall of Truth in the afterlife.

The sun and air are both ruled by Amun (Amun-Ra). Patron of the city of Thebes, he was one of the most powerful and well-liked gods of ancient Egypt. He was worshiped alongside Amun, Mut, and Khonsu as a member of the Theban Triad. Originally a minor fertility god, but at some periods the supreme ruler of the gods. He was regarded as Egypt's most potent deity by the time of the New Kingdom, and worship of him was almost exclusively monotheistic. Even other deities were viewed at this time as just facets of Amun. The position of God's Wife of Amun, bestowed upon royal women, was practically on par with that of the pharaoh, and his priesthood was the most powerful in all of Egypt.

Anubis is a dead god who is connected to embalming. Father of Qebhet and the son of Nephthys and Osiris. Anubis is typically shown as a man with a dog or jackal-like head and a staff. He participated in the ceremony of the Weighing of the Heart of the Soul in the hereafter and directed the souls of the deceased to the Hall of Truth. He was most likely the first God of the Dead until Osiris assumed that position, at which point he was designated as Osiris' son.

God of chaos, storms, battle, and plague is Set (Seth). His name is sometimes translated as "Destroyer" and "Instigator of Confusion." He is the model for later Christian Devil iconography and is portrayed as a red beast with cloven hooves and a forked tail. Originally a hero-god, Set expelled the serpent Apep (Apophis) from the sun god's barge and killed it every night. He was a god of the desert who carried the pernicious winds of the barren plains to the luxuriant Nile Valley and was connected to otherworldly places and people. His consorts included Taweret, the benevolent, protective goddess of childbirth and fertility, as well as Anat and Astarte, two alien deities who were both linked with battle and fertility. Although Set is frequently described as "evil" and did exhibit many negative traits, the ancient Egyptians did not see him as a symbol of evil or darkness. He was viewed as more of an essential counterbalance to gods like Osiris and Horus, who stood for all that was honorable and good, fertility, vitality, and eternity. In the Myth of Osiris, Set kills his brother in order to steal the throne, making him the first murderer in history. Osiris is brought back to life by Isis, but he enters the underworld as the Lord of the Dead since he is lacking something. Horus, the son of Osiris born to Isis, grows up to fight for the throne. In the literature The Contendings of Horus and Set, their conflicts, which lasted for eighty years, are recorded. In one account, Isis pronounced Horus to be the true monarch, and in the other, Neith banished Set to the desert realms.

Waset (Wosret), also known as "The Powerful Female One," was a guardian deity of Thebes. She represented the city, also known as "Waset," in all its guises. She was once a part of Hathor, but by the Middle Kingdom, she had developed her own unique personality and iconography (c. 2040-1782 BCE). She is pictured as a female carrying the Was scepter, an ankh, a staff decorated with ribbons, as well as a bow and arrows and an axe, which stand for Thebes's military prowess.

Sothis: A representation of Sirius, often known as the "dog star," whose arrival signaled the annual flooding of the Nile. In the Predynastic Period (c. 6000-3150 BCE), she was revered as a cow-goddess and connected to

Sirius. She was married to Sah, who represented the constellation Orion and was a fusion of Osiris and Isis. She served as the protector in this capacity because she was Sopdu's mother. She was also connected to Satis, who was Khnum's consort and was associated with the flooding of the Nile. Later images of Sothis portray her as a lady wearing the White Crown of Upper Egypt, with horns on her head or feathers, and a five-pointed star above her. Early representations of Sothis show her as a cow with a plant between her horns. She began to identify more and more with Isis, and until she was entirely subsumed into that deity. In a manuscript of The Lamentations of Isis and Nephthys from the Ptolemaic Dynasty (323–30 BCE), Isis refers to herself as Sothis, demonstrating how assimilation was nearly complete at that time.

Osiris is one of Egypt's most well-known and enduring deities. He is the Lord and Judge of the Dead, one of the First Five gods to be born of Nut at the beginning of creation. His name is an allusion to strength or might. A fertility deity at first, Osiris gained popularity and power thanks to the Osiris Myth, in which he is killed by his brother Set, revived by his wife Isis, gives birth to the sky god Horus, and enters the underworld as the Judge of the Dead.

Horus was a primitive avian god who rose to prominence in ancient Egypt. Horus, a god of the sun, sky, and power, was connected to the Egyptian ruler as early as the First Dynasty (c. 3150-2890 BCE). Horus the Elder, one of the first five gods born at the beginning of creation, and Horus the Younger, the son of Osiris and Isis, are the two avian deities most commonly associated with the name. Horus the Younger rose to prominence as the Osiris Myth gained in popularity, making him one of Egypt's most revered deities. Horus is brought up by his mother in the Delta wetlands following the murder of Osiris by his brother Set in the narrative. When he reaches adulthood, he faces up against his uncle for the kingdom and prevails, bringing peace to the land. With a few notable exceptions, every Egyptian ruler identified both in life and in death with Horus and Osiris. Horus was said to have given his

people all good things through the
king, who was seen as the god's living
embodiment. He is often pictured as a
man with a hawk's head, but there are
numerous more representations of
him. The hawk and the Eye of Horus
are his emblems.

Chapter 3

Egyptian architecture

Obelisks, battered walls, pylon-towers, pyramids, cavetto (or gorge) cornices, large columns with lotus, papyrus, palm, and other capitals, hypostyle halls, courts, enormous processional axes (called dromos), flanked by sphinxes, stylized sculpture, and hieroglyphs were all features of ancient Egyptian architecture, which was primarily that of the monumental temple and tomb. It has a columnar and trabeated style of architecture. Imhotep planned the early stone-built Saqqara funeral complex, which had a stepped pyramid, a processional hall with engaged columns that were reeded and fluted, courts, and a large wall enclosing the entire structure. The smooth-sided type, which the Gizeh pyramids (mid-third millennium BC) are examples of, replaced the stepped type as the dominant type of pyramid. The large temple complex at Der-el-Bahari, built around the middle of the second millennium BC, had three main levels that were reached by ramps and long façades of straightforward square columns. These features had a significant impact on Neo-Classicism and rational architecture in the twentieth century. Around the same time, the temple complexes of Karnak and Luxor were also begun, and even now, their remains are spectacular. The Philae and Edfu temples are among the several structures from the

Graeco-Roman era (332 BCE to 395 BCE) that still stand today.

Many Egyptian characteristics were assimilated by the Hellenistic Greek cultures and by the Roman Empire. Neo-Classicism, Art Deco, Rational architecture, and Post-Modernism drew on Ancient Egyptian motifs. The rock-cut tombs at Beni-Hasan, for example, include proto-Doric columns.

Flat roofs, enormous walls covered in hieroglyphic and pictorial carving, post and lintel construction, and constructions like the mastaba, obelisk, pylon, and the Pyramids are all characteristics of architecture that has been produced from 3000 BC. Homes were constructed using baked bricks or clay. Features of home architecture were replicated in tombs and temples, but on a far larger scale and with more durable materials. Imhotep was perhaps the greatest builder of his day.

Amazing Ancient Egyptian Monuments

The Giza Great Pyramids. The Giza Great Pyramids.

In Abu Simbel. Ramesses II's Colossus in Abu Simbel.

Giza's Great Sphinx.

Temple of Karnak.

The Hatshepsut Mortuary Temple.

The Red Pyramid of Sneferu with the
Bent Pyramid.

Egyptian Temple.

The Djoser Step Pyramid.

Chapter 4

Egyptian art

Ma'at, a harmonious idea that originated at the beginning of creation and supported the universe, served as the foundation of Egyptian society. Because it depicts the ideal world of the gods, all Egyptian art is predicated on perfect equilibrium. The artwork was envisioned and produced with the intention of serving a purpose, just as these gods supplied all wonderful gifts for humanity. Egyptian art was always primarily intended for practical purposes. No matter how exquisitely made a statue may have been, its main function was to house a god or spirit. Although an amulet would have been created with aesthetic attractiveness in mind, protection was the main consideration. The shape of tomb murals, temple tableaus, residence, and palace gardens were all designed to serve a significant purpose; frequently, this purpose was to serve as a reminder of the ephemeral nature of life and the importance of both individual and group stability.

From the very beginning, Egyptian art was infused with the value of balance, which is represented through symmetry. This value is established by Predynastic Period rock art and is fully developed and achieved in Early Dynastic Period of Egypt (c. 3150 - c. 2613 BCE). The work known as The Narmer Palette, which was produced between 3200 and 3000 BCE to commemorate the unification of Upper and Lower Egypt under King Narmer, is the pinnacle of this era's artistic achievement (c. 3150 BCE). The tale of the great king's victory over his adversaries and how the gods supported and approved of his actions is told through a sequence of carvings on a siltstone slab shaped as a chevron shield. The story of unification and the celebration of the king is pretty evident, despite the fact that some of the pictures on the palette are challenging to decipher.

Narmer, who represents the divine might of the bull (perhaps the Apis Bull), is seen in a triumphal march while clad in the crowns of Upper and Lower Egypt. Two men are seen grappling with entangled creatures below him, which are frequently understood as standing for Upper and Lower Egypt (though this view is contested and there seems no justification for it). On the back, the gods may be seen cheering the monarch on as he defeats his opponents. These scenes are all expertly carved in low-raised relief.

When creating the pyramid complex for King Djoser at the end of the Early Dynastic Period, architect Imhotep (c. 2667-2600 BCE) would apply this technique rather well (c. 2670 BCE). The buildings feature beautifully carved lotus flowers, papyrus plants, and the djed sign in both high relief and low relief. By this time, stoneworkers had mastered the technique for producing life-size statues that were three-dimensional. One of this era's outstanding pieces of art is the statue of Djoser.

www.ingramcontent.com/pod-product-compliance
Lightning Source LLC
Chambersburg PA
CBHW060925130726
48001CB00006B/2426